A DRESS, A RING,
PROMISES TO SELF

an unconventional wedding planner for one

by Sara Sharpe

Library of Congress ISBN 1468068873
EAN-13 is 978-1468068870

Book design by DJ Anderson

Printed in the United States of America
2nd edition

on the porch with the kitten, who I couldn't help but
feed last night when sleep wouldn't come,

i think of sara.

i think of her recent ritual, private and sacred save for a few
details–

a dress, a ring, promises to self.

she tells trenna late one night while I sit in the kitchen with B,

i married my self.

explanation enough.

mmmhhm, says Trenna…

by paige la grone babcock

For Trenna and Jacob

A DRESS, A RING, PROMISES TO SELF

CONTENTS

PROLOGUE

This beloved little book has had a special place on my personal book shelf for over ten years. (I performed my own ceremony in 2001, and wrote about it a few years later.) Over the years, I've offered it to friends, now and again, as a gift. Beyond that, however, I had no real plan to distribute it widely. That is, until Elizabeth got hold of it.

At some point last year, I gave a copy to Elizabeth Jackson, who is the daughter of a dear friend (and who is also a dear friend in her own right. Elizabeth's photo/photos appear in this book on several occasions – she is both model and photographer). Elizabeth fell in love with the book, and encouraged me to make it readily available. On a whim, I wrote a blurb about it on facebook in December 2011, though I didn't expect much to come of it.

Something did come of it, however. In short, I sold so many books in December (in digital, notebook, and handmade form) that I essentially took a month off work to fill orders.

There are, I believe, personal reasons that this little book has jumped off of my shelf and out into the world (that being another story for another day). Beyond that, however, it is my belief that this book represents an idea whose time has come. This is not to imply that the idea of making a commitment to love, honor and care for oneself so that one might better love, honor and care for others is a new one; it isn't. But ritualizing the commitment – setting the intention and concretizing it – is somewhat new to most folks and, I think, valuable.

A quick note about the lack of diversity in these pages: all of the photographs (with only one exception) are of young, white women. I celebrate them, each and every one, but confess that this was not my original intent. A photo shoot that I tried for months to put together never materialized (everyone, it seems, is as busy as I am) and so, in the end, I chose pre-existing photos. My options, while brilliant, were limited in this regard. It is my great hope that someday I can include photos of ceremonies conducted by women (and men!) of all ages, colors, body types etc.

This book is for and about you (even if you don't see yourself reflected in the photographs!) That said, I'd be remiss if I failed to mention my hope that your commitment to live a fully realized life positively affects not only your immediate family, as it must, but also the world beyond your family.

Recently I learned that a group of seven women is planning a collective ceremony, inspired by this book. To them I wrote, "The world needs you; not some watered down version of you, but a healthy, whole, fully expressed and passionately alive you."

To that I would add - at great risk of getting unnecessarily (but only briefly) heavy handed - the following: The world needs you, indeed - partially because every day we are made more aware of unsustainable stress points on our planet. Around the globe, one child dies every 17 seconds due to malnutrition, 90 percent of war casualties are civilians (almost half are children), and over 50 countries currently recruit children under 18 into their armed forces. In this country, 16.7 million children live in food insecure households and, according to the National Children's Alliance, in 2011 alone, 95,120 children reported sexual abuse, and 25,414 children reported physical abuse. And so on.

With all that in mind, I encourage you, with all the passion I can muster, to celebrate and take seriously this opportunity to heal, to grow, to commit to feeling and being your best, not only for yourselves, but for your own children, and for children the world over. We can care for them effectively only when we've learned to care for ourselves at least as well.

Wild hope,
Sara

INTRODUCTION

"Making a commitment to honor one's self is an absolute prerequisite to marriage in the traditional sense. And if you're already married? It's certainly not too late…"

In the summer of 2001, I married my self. In the beautiful town of Balsam, North Carolina, I bought a long white dress, a huge bundle of flowers, and a ring that I wear to this day. I stayed up all night writing a list of promises to my self, building a temporary altar at which to perform the sacred event, and decorating my cheerful, purple room at the Balsam Mountain Inn. The following night I donned my dress and, with a home-made wreath of flowers in my hair, tearfully made a commitment to honor my self, first and foremost, henceforth.

As one who had spent years performing "daily acts of self crucifixion," in the words of Emmanuel (see page 9), which usually took the form of refusing to listen to my gut and putting everyone else's needs before my own - this was a radically important paradigm shift. Additionally, it was, and is, a commitment that I take very seriously, and one that I believe to be an absolute prerequisite to marriage in the traditional sense.

I wish this sort of ceremony for every woman (and man for that matter) regardless of age, sexual orientation or marital status. Few would argue with the notion that it is hard, if not impossible, to love, honor and care for another if one does not first love, honor and care for one's self. Some things deserve to be elevated to ritual status, and making the sort of commitment described herein is, in my humble opinion, just such a thing.

I encourage you to use this book as a guide. Think of it as an unconventional wedding planner. Take two days, two months or two years to plan your ceremony, but plan it. Construct your altar in an exotic location, or your own backyard; make it a private affair, or send out invitations… It's your day, your journey – and the ritual can be as simple or as elaborate as you wish. The only rule is that every aspect of your ceremony be an accurate reflection of you. This is the time to be utterly self-indulgent.

Most importantly, a commitment ceremony such as this one provides a tangible opportunity to begin (or continue) to heal the past, imagine the future, and to construct – first on paper and then in your relationships – boundaries that will keep you safe, rituals that will keep you connected to the Divine, and language that will enable you to communicate your deepest desires.

WHY AND WHEN TO USE THIS BOOK

"You live your lives within the models you were given, until a moment arises when you realize that for all your goodwill and excellent behavior, you are empty. You touch a longing that nothing in your world can answer. You hear a voice calling you to something totally unfamiliar, 'Be who you are.'"
~Emmanuel

WHY TO USE THIS BOOK

If current divorce rates are any indication, we view marriage differently than did our parents (or grandparents, depending on your age). If marriage was once considered a lifetime commitment, it is often now a temporary (albeit important) foray into the world of partnership, with all its trials and tribulations. While this trend is often considered a tragic casualty wrought by the self-absorbed, commitment-phobic ME generation, I tend to think it an inevitable part of our collective growth. As self absorbed as the Boomers and Gen-Xers have seemed these past few decades, we have laid important offerings at the sacred altar of marriage.

I'm not at all convinced, for instance, that it is any better to stay in a dead marriage than it is to leave one. Surely our generation deserves some credit for breaking the confines of traditional values that, with their emphasis on commitment above all else, forced countless numbers of men and women to stifle their own personal growth and to live with the inherent dishonesty that comes with putting on a happy face for the sake of the children, the community, etc.

> You formulate yourselves in tiny but continuous acts of self-crucifixion, shaping yourselves to who you believe you are required to be.

If, in the last century, we have gone from one extreme to another (extreme emphasis on commitment versus extreme emphasis on discovering and nurturing the authentic self), it could be argued that the extremes have been necessary in order to strike a balance between the two – part and parcel of finding the middle road at long last.

With all that in mind, then, it is my great hope that future generations will learn that it is indeed possible to evolve personally within the context of a conscious, evolving partnership. Additionally, I hope that our children, mine included, will choose their life partners with far more self-awareness than we did, and that they will view their commitments with all the seriousness they deserve.

This, I would argue, will only be possible if we take up William Shakespeare's challenge of old: "To thine own self be true."

The trouble in marriage, more often than not, comes when its very foundation is built on false pretenses.

"The self was taught that definitions of being good, being worthy, noble, and honorable all had to be sifted through the opinion of another. This is not a criticism of parenting. It is simply the way it is, and it serves a purpose.

At each moment throughout your day, such choices are made. They go something like this: 'Who shall I be right now? The one my mother wants me to be? The one my father wants me to be? The one my brothers and sisters hope I'm not? The one my lover thinks I am? The one my children demand I be? Who shall I be?'

Because this practice of choosing is so automatic, it seldom even ruffles the edges of your active consciousness. And so you formulate yourselves in tiny but continuous acts of self-crucifixion, shaping yourselves to who you believe you are required to be. You need to become aware of this habit.

You live your lives within the models you were given, until a moment arises when you realize that for all your goodwill and excellent behavior, you are empty. You touch a longing that nothing in your world can answer. You hear a voice calling you to something totally unfamiliar, 'Be who you are.'"

Emmanuel
Emmanuel's Book 11

If the internal command, "Be who you are" makes itself known two, ten, twenty years into marriage, and if this increasingly authentic self differs greatly from the wife, husband, mother, father etc. your family has known all these years, the results can be messy at best - especially if your immediate family members are quite comfortable with the self, authentic or not, with which you have presented them and upon whom the familial structure is built.

In truth, I speak with some experience – for this is exactly what happened to me and my family, years ago. At some point during this wrenching process, I wrote about a conversation I might have had with and about my highest Self:

> She is beautiful. That is the first thing I notice about her. She embodies the beauty that results from full expression and a total lack of fear; the beauty of one who LIVES! And as she approaches she is laughing at me good naturedly, this dear part of herself who insists on hanging onto the rock...
>
> "You look frightened, Sara," she laughs. The voice, like the laugh, is clear as a bell. Relaxed. Easy.

"Oh, but I have every reason to be frightened," I say, the least bit offended that she would laugh at me right off. This is, after all, rather serious to me from where I'm hanging, and she must know this. "This is change on every level at once! This is leaving everything I know for... well, for what? I can see nothing you know, and why would one leave something for nothing..." I ramble on from there – as good a place as any – about the void and the black hole and the future I say I can't see (knowing all the while that she knows better.) "O.K.," I correct. "I can see it. Where I might go, what I would do, who I could be. But I can't imagine how I might get there! The journey from here to there! There is the blind spot. In the meantime, what if I have to take a job that I hate just to make the money I need to barely scrape by? I have no degree, you know, and limited skills. The jobs that are available to me are mindless! Uninteresting! And I will have to live in a small yet very expensive house that couldn't possibly be as perfect and as comfortable as this one! And how could any of this possibly move me in the direction of my dream?"

> The path is there and it will reveal itself one step at a time.

She sighs a bit, my stronger self, sorry to have to tell me what I already know. "Remember, Sara. You need not struggle unless you think you must. Struggle and dissatisfaction are based on a misunderstanding of the universe. Beauty, abundance, the image you hold in your mind (you know the one) is yours for the asking. In fact, it's what you came for. Of course you can't see the path that will lead you there. Where would be the joy of daily discovery if you could? Where would be the exercise in faith? You can trust that the path is there and that it will reveal itself one step at a time. Keep the end in sight. Pray daily for the next step which, if you don't insist on making it difficult, must always be more beautiful than the last. I'll take your hand and we'll go..."

It was nice, this – the part of me that remembered, reminding the part of me that forgot.

"I'm good with the big picture," I remind her. "It's the reality of the day to day that trips me up... My husband reminds me of this all the time..."

My husband.

I look up to see the flash of pain that grips me pass through her as well, but instead of pain I see her smile. Still. Different. Not amused, now. Tender...

I start slowly. "My husband says 'we' is a choice. I say 'we' either is or isn't on some fundamental level. In any case, we must find out because we are, at this point, hurting each other more than we are helping. A separation would be the easiest way to discover these things; the fastest way. And by this point it is what I want. I can see that it is the best thing for me... for my husband.

My husband.

"But please," I beg, for what I'm not sure, and I can feel the tears start to come. "The thought of not being with Husband the familiar! Husband the kind, Husband the joy, Husband my partner, for better or worse, for the past ten years! How I love him! True it may be that, try as we might, he may never be what I need – and vice versa – but how I love him. How I would mourn the loss if he were not here..."

"Damn you for smiling!" And my tears turn to sobs, damn it, because I had planned to show her that she was not so far removed from me, this strong and knowing Sara who could see past the illusion. "How can you smile in the face of death? It is a ripping away, tearing apart, excruciatingly painful, wrenching, death! Oh, what father does not want to live every moment with his beloved children? What father wouldn't die one thousand deaths knowing that he will no longer kiss his babies to sleep each and every night, wake to them in the morning, come home to them in the afternoon? What kind of mother would allow such a separation? Pain, pain, pain, pain for everyone involved – and at my insistence. Pain for the father's mother, the mother's mother, the fathers, the friends, the brothers... and for what again?"

I can't seem to remember in the face of such pain and I am paralyzed again. The strength is gone, clarity a thing of the past.

I don't look at her now because if I see through my tears that she is smiling still, I will hate her. There is nothing she or anyone can say to relieve me. Nothing she can say that will comfort me; nothing to move me forward. I am not ready. She has come too soon.

Perhaps.

Eventually, however, when I was ready, I did move forward – past the naïve belief that with enough positive thinking my life would be devoid of struggle, and out of a situation that didn't allow for much self actualization. In my case, this meant granting myself the freedom to make nearly two decades worth of "mistakes," in large measure. And while thirteen years of disempowering relationships was NOT what I had in mind when I left my marriage, my learning curve was necessary in the big scheme of things. Thirteen years ago I didn't know any better, and now I do. Had I stayed where I was, I still wouldn't know any better.

***

Incidentally, I have a history of attracting and being attracted to particularly dynamic men, including my terrific ex-husband. And in the two relationships I've been in since my marriage, I was involved with men who were both fully in their power (professionally, at least). Though the work they did was very different - one was an artist, the other an athlete - they were, both of them, brilliant at what they did - brilliant and beautiful to watch, however beautiful they were or were not in other ways.

I mention this not to hint at the less than interesting history of my relationships, but to offer an observation that circles back to our goal of self actualization and making a commitment to one's self. If dynamism

> For anyone not yet fully in their own power/ passion, there is a real tendency to be drawn into the power of someone who is.

was one thing these two men had in common, the other was the dizzying number of people (women, mostly, but men too) who organized their lives around them. The way in which this happened was sometimes different, but the reasons were always the same: power and/or passion, on some level. For anyone not yet fully in their own power/passion, there is a real tendency to be drawn into the power of someone who is. (Take it from one who knows.) This tendency is hazardous in that those who wield such power are seldom healthy and balanced enough to keep from abusing it in one way or another (at least in my experience.) This tendency is not only hazardous . . . at times, it can be downright dangerous.

We see examples of this dynamic all around us – think charismatic politicians, preachers, celebrities, corporate execs etc. – and the very many people who flock to them. Additionally, and just as importantly, it is crucial to realize that this same dynamic, on a smaller scale, is very common in relationships of all kinds – even and especially romantic ones. While this power dynamic can shift from one person to another throughout the course of a relationship, there is typically one person who wields more power than the other; not because she or he has demanded it, but because it has been freely given.

These symbiotic relationships, even if they aren't the dangerous variety, are never healthy, as common as they are. (We should also note that they are as radically unfair to the person on whom you're dependent as they are unfair to you.) Furthermore, if such relationships fail to evolve, they inevitably end in heartache. As well they should. Whatever the relationship (romantic, professional, or familial), if you're dependent on someone else to provide you with a feeling of power or passion – or excitement, or status, or security, or safety, or absolution etc., – and IF you fail to take responsibility for yourself, you're likely headed for a crash. But don't despair. The crash, while brutal, is a gift beyond measure. There is no clearer indicator of the ways in which, and the degree to which, you've given away your power. You will recover. And, hopefully, (with the help of this book, perhaps) you won't make the same mistake in the same way next time.

A crash isn't necessary, of course. With enough awareness, even the most codependent relationship can be brought into balance. But at the very least, I want you to be aware of this sort of codependency. As long as it's in play, you've no chance of experiencing either self actualization or a true partnership. Ultimately, I want you to make a commitment to never again look to someone else for power. My wish for you is a life that is fully expressive, passionate, exceptional, and free of addiction and codependency. The commitment you make to yourself, with the help of this book, will set the intention. Set it, and follow through.

WHEN TO USE THIS BOOK

If you are young and just starting to explore yourself and your world, independent of your immediate family, welcome to a grand and glorious adventure. This is your time to discover what good, worthy, noble and honorable mean to YOU – not to your parents, not to your teachers, not to your friends – but to you. This is the time to follow your heart, chase your dreams, and establish habits of extreme self care. This is your time to learn to respect yourself absolutely, and to then demand this same respect from anyone and everyone who comes into your life henceforth.

Moreover, this is the time to realize that this should not be a temporary adventure - to be conducted just after leaving home, just before settling down – but a way of life. Learn that; carry that knowledge with you always, and you will enter into all subsequent relationships with the crucial self awareness that those of us who came before you wish we had had.

If you are mining the depths of your soul self for this first time - or for the first time in a long time – and you are currently in a partnership, I urge you to proceed with caution. It is easy to shift blame in such instances, and outright rebellion can be tempting. The truth is, you, and you alone, are ultimately responsible for the "tiny but continuous acts of self-crucifixion" that have left you less than whole.

An additional red flag – extramarital affairs sometimes offer what, on the surface, seem to be the most direct route to the passionate, alive, authentic self that has been either buried or unknown. To go down this road is almost always a mistake.

Whether single or married, if you are serious about this journey of self-discovery, the last thing you want to do is rely on someone else to take you down that road. I beg you, resist the urge, which can be all but irresistible, and realize that any new love affair, at this point, ought to be self contained. You are beautiful, sensuous, unique, powerful, and you don't need anyone else to convince you that this is so. To rely on another for this awakening is to make the same mistake you've made in the past.

Walk away. There will be plenty of time for partnership in the future; partnership in which you can offer a healthy, joyous, whole self.

> You are beautiful, sensuous, unique, powerful, and you don't need anyone else to convince you that this is so.

14

If you have recently been through a painful breakup, recognize that this is a good time, once the shock and near paralysis give way, to begin planning your ceremony - slowly, carefully, as part of the healing process. What better way to release the past and to call back those parts of yourself that were lost, as they so often are, in a doomed relationship?

For those of you who still mourn a lost love, remember: you don't have lots of time to waste feeling regretful. The relationship lasted for precisely as long as it was supposed to last and not a minute longer.

Keeping "your eye on the truth," as Carolyn Myss writes, and remembering "that everything and everyone in your life is there by contract to assist in your spiritual maturation" has been of some comfort to me when I've been tempted to feel overwhelmed by the sense of loss that accompanies a changed relationship.

Grieve fully, get professional help if you need it, write out your anger, seek the company of good friends, pray regularly if you're spiritually inclined, help someone in need, give thanks and keep moving.

If you have been betrayed, lied to, and/or left for another, take heed; you called this experience to yourself for a reason, and you have a choice: you can be relentlessly bitter and broken (you'll be both for a while), or you can recognize and honor the lesson, learn from it, forgive (eventually), and rise from the ashes.

I don't mean to be crass, honestly; I don't mean to be harsh. But please don't waste a minute on useless comparisons, unhealthy obsessions, and prolonged agony. If you have been betrayed by another, don't dare betray yourself; instead, look to God (or whatever you choose to call Divinity) and in the same breath, look to yourself for yourself. This is another time to avoid jumping into a new relationship. Instead, plan your ceremony. In so doing you will find, if you're patient enough, a Divine being quite capable of putting the entire experience in perspective. You will find, I assure you, a beautiful, fierce, powerful creature capable of greatness heretofore unimagined.

Settle for nothing less.

HOW TO USE THIS BOOK

This is the time to be utterly self indulgent.

This book is for and about you. It is both a planner and a journal with a very specific purpose; to help you plan your commitment ceremony – your marriage to your self.

While our model is the traditional wedding ceremony (in all its ritual beauty, joy and seriousness), don't be constrained by any one idea of what a commitment ceremony should look like. I've already mentioned a group of women who are in the process of planning a collective ceremony. They plan to circle up and to then read their promises aloud to each other. I hadn't thought of this myself, but I love the idea!

Whatever you decide to do, I suggest putting serious thought into your ring, your dress or suit, the location at which you'll perform the sacred event, your flowers, invitations, etc.

This is the time, as I stated earlier, to be utterly self indulgent. Love to shop? Have a brilliant time searching for your dress/suit. Hit your favorite boutiques at home, or take a special weekend trip to a different location and look for something special. Feeling creative? Design and make your own; if you don't sew, design it and have someone else make it – or hire someone to help you create your very own work of art and get sewing lessons in the bargain. Same with your ring, the invitations, the altar; buy them, make them, or have them made. When the time comes you can buy flowers or collect them outside…

Note: If you take a more formal approach to your ceremony and/or choose to hire help, the notes following each section – as well as those in the appendix – will help you keep track of who's doing what, when and for how much!

Use this book to cut and paste pictures that capture the image you have of your special day. Use it to keep all the requisite information in one place. Use this book to write about what you want, both generally and specifically, remembering that your commitment ceremony is not the end all and be all; rather it is the beginning of a joyous, lifetime commitment. Let your planning reflect that greater purpose.

Dream, create, and plan on these pages, but take your dreams, your creation and your planning seriously; set a definite date and follow through with your commitment.

FLOWERS

Fennel – Worthy of all praise
Hyacinth – Play
Lily of the Valley – Return to happiness

I love flowers. When I can't afford to buy them, and even when I can, I often take to the woods and bring back whatever strikes my fancy.

I once built a bed out of huge, fallen tree limbs and twisted vine that I covered in whatever was blooming – tea roses in spring, honeysuckle in the summer and holly (replete with red berries) in winter. Going to sleep surrounded by the scent of fresh flowers is glorious beyond measure; seductive, comforting, fairy-like. When I grew tired of fresh flowers, I adorned my homemade bed with beautiful dried ones.

If I were to plan my ceremony again, I would construct a handmade altar covered in flowers and candles. I would buy as many as I could afford and gather as many as I could find. Few things are more fun than searching the woods for beautiful fallen branches, vines, colorful leaves and wild flowers. Then, too, I love spending time in beautiful flower shops and, if money were no object, I might consider hiring help.

For my own ceremony, I bought flowers and made a homemade wreath for my hair. As well, I made a beautiful bouquet and decorated my small altar with whatever was left over, along with some sweet smelling candles. (The purple walls in my room at the Balsam Mountain Inn were a perfect backdrop for the arrangement.)

Much has been written about the language of flowers. If you're interested, there is plenty of information out there as to flowers and their meanings. The information is not always consistent, and you may or may not care what a flower means according to Lady Mary Wortley Montagu (a celebrated letter-writer and society poet who, in 1716, interpreted the meanings of some plants, flowers, and spices).

But if you're interested, here's a list to get you started:

FLOWERS AND THEIR MEANINGS

Bay leaf - Strength
Bittersweet -Truth
Carnation (in general) –
    Health and energy;
    fascination; woman
    love
Cattail – Peace; prosperity
Chamomile – Patience
Chrysanthemum (white)
    – Truth
Crocus – Cheerfulness;
    abuse not
Clover – Good luck
Daffodil – Respect
Dandelion – Wishes
    come true

Eucalyptus – Protection
Fennel – Worthy of all
    praise
Hyacinth – Play
Lily of the Valley –
    Return to happiness
Magnolia – Sweetness;
    beauty; love of nature
Mint – Protection from
    illness
Orchid – Mature charm
Pansy – Thoughts, love
Pine – Hope
Violet – Modesty, calms
    tempers
Yarrow – Health, healing

20

NOTES

DRESS

...the dress I chose was a little big for me. This didn't matter in the least; it was long, white, free-spirited, and it made me feel beautiful.

As a young person, I genuinely didn't care much for fashion, and wore what was comfortable as opposed to what looked great. As I recall, even for my senior prom I couldn't bring myself to think about what I would wear until the night before the big event. I remember running to the mall near closing time, buying a simple, strapless pink thing, and borrowing shoes from a friend on the way home. Those were the good old days.

As I grew older, my relationship with clothes grew more complicated – tied up, as it was, with my self esteem. My issues with clothing had nothing to do with a simple compulsion to dress according to the latest fashion; quite the opposite, actually. I was afraid to dress up. My friends and I were young activists involved in social justice work, and fashion was the last thing we were supposed to be thinking about. It took me a long time to discover that it was as damaging to my self esteem to dress down for fear of being judged as it was to dress up. Either way, I was dressing for someone other than myself.

There is a lot to be said for keeping fashion in perspective and, when it comes to clothing, it is indeed possible to combine both aesthetics and ethics. (Check out the Edun line at Saks Fifth Avenue, or visit greenloop.com.) It is important, however, not to go out of your way not to be a "clothes person" if you genuinely love clothes.

Shopping for my dress was a joyous proposition. I was absolutely free to choose whatever I wanted with no input from anyone else. For me, the choice had much more to do with how I felt than how I looked and, in fact, the dress I chose was a little big for me. This didn't matter in the least; it was long, white, free-spirited, and it made me feel beautiful.

If you sew, get out your old sewing machine and create a one-of-a-kind wedding dress. Unlike a traditional wedding, there will be no critical audience per se, and no mothers to please. You'll either be by yourself or you'll be surrounded by people who will accept you as you are, no questions asked. So if you want to adorn yourself with yards of sheer white material and fresh flowers, go for it. Or design a tailored work of art and have something made. Or shop at your favorite boutique. (Men, this goes for you too).

NOTES

RING

In shopping for my ring I was looking, of course, for a tangible, long-lasting symbol of my promises to my self – one that would be a constant reminder.

As I researched stones and their meanings online, I found that no two websites were alike. Apparently stones, even more than flowers, have different meanings depending on who you ask.

I'm not even sure what the stone in my ring is, though I was told when I bought it and I've been told once since then. Frankly, I've never been interested enough to commit it to memory – I bought it because it was a handmade thing of beauty and I loved it instantly. In shopping for my ring I was looking, of course, for a tangible, long-lasting symbol of my promises to myself – one that would be a constant reminder.

I recently ran into a woman who bought one of the original, handmade copies of this book. She showed me the ring she had chosen to represent her commitment to herself - a gorgeous, thick, handcrafted silver ring, replete with a diamond. She proudly wears it on her middle finger, which she flips up unceremoniously every time she shows it off! Having just gotten out of a difficult relationship, this gives her a feeling of empowerment (hey, whatever works) and a good laugh every time she does it.

My entire commitment ceremony was conceived, prepared, and carried out within a three-day span. I got lucky and found the perfect dress and ring in the same town on the same day, the likelihood of which surprises me in retrospect. It helps that I was in Waynesboro, North Carolina, which is a gorgeous, mountain town full of artisans clearly inspired by their surroundings. Much of the art in Waynesboro seems somehow to have harnessed the wild beauty and quiet, massive strength that permeate the air in and around the Blue Ridge Parkway. It is no accident that this was the backdrop for my ceremony – I needed to weave the strength of my surroundings into my commitment and self. This same beauty and strength found its way into the symbols I chose, and both my ring and my dress perfectly expressed the unique and free-spirited style I craved.

When it comes to your ring, once again, the rules aren't set in stone. (No pun intended). Design one and have it made, buy a gorgeous diamond from your favorite jeweler, or dig one out of a Cracker Jack box. (Actually I would encourage something more long-lasting than that, but it's up to you; it is, of course, the promise more than the symbol that matters.)

Incidentally, a few years after my divorce, I had the diamond from my wedding ring removed and put into a simple, elegant setting that I wear around my neck. This, too, was an important gesture for me personally. I wanted my children, Trenna and Jacob, to understand that though my relationship with their father had changed, our love and respect for each other (and all that we learned together) remained. And so it does. Symbolically then, the setting changed, but the diamond was and is as brilliant and beautiful as before.

NOTES

PROMISES

If you have surrendered your self to others in ways that have diminished you,
reclaim that self now and, with your promises,
sing flesh back onto your bones.

It all boils down to the promises, really.

I wrote mine in one, impassioned sitting. They spilled out onto the page in a way that was fierce, un-controlled and, so far as I can tell, thorough. As a written document they're not pretty, and they could certainly stand some editing. (And I doubt they make sense to anyone but me!) But I have never re-written them, nor will I. They came from a deep place and I know better.

I had lost so much of myself through the years – my voice, my art, my beauty and power – and I had amassed so much, SO MUCH fear, that I couldn't function fully. I had also carried with me heaps and heaps of guilt and shame. I had a lot to discover and rediscover and even more to release.

When I look back at my promises to my self I see, essentially, reclamation, release, a Divine act of co-creation and a supreme act of forgiveness.

Write your promises when you feel so led. They may come all at once, or they may come slowly, over days, weeks, or even months.

As a starting point, you might ask yourself the following questions:

◊   What are some of the ways that you've "sold yourself out" over the years?
◊   Have you failed to speak up for yourself, on occasion?
◊   Do you have a habit of hiding your real feelings so as not to make the people around you angry?
◊   Do you have a gut feeling that you are ignoring?
◊   Do you put up with the bad behavior of others for fear of being alone?
◊   Are you living a life that is fully expressive? Passionate? If not, why not?
◊   Are you settling in any capacity?
◊   Are you currently in a relationship that is abusive in any way? If so, why do you stay in the relationship? What are you afraid of?
◊   Are you speaking your truth fearlessly? If not, why not?
◊   Do you have a dream that you have let languish? If so, why? Etc.

In other words, think about ways in which you have abandoned your self, and make a commitment to stop. To re-frame that in a positive way, PROMISE yourself that you will work hard, henceforth, to speak your truth, breathe life into your dreams, stand up for yourself, hold out for that someone who treats you the way you deserve to be treated, take better care of yourself physically and/or spiritually, etc.

THE WORLD NEEDS YOU; not some watered down version of you, as I've said before, but a healthy, whole, fully expressed and passionately alive you. Your family needs you in this way, as does your community, as does your world.

Some suggestions, if I may be so bold: If you are abused in any way, by anyone, verbally and/or physically, promise your self – to whom you now commit absolutely – that the abuse can and must stop. Once you have made this promise, seek whatever help you need immediately. If you have surrendered your self to others in ways that have diminished you, reclaim that self now and, with your promises, sing flesh back onto your bones. If you have found a true and good partner with whom you want to share your life, promise to nurture your fundamental, essential relationship with self, first and foremost. Few things do more for a partnership.

Finally, recognize your promises as a sacred and focused starting point. As with all commitments, seeing them through takes soulful tenacity and endurance.

My promises, for whatever they're worth to you, begin on the following page.

I promise
I am
Possessed of and safe in my beauty and power

Wide open as she on the hill in the wind

A new season

Safe and protected in all corners of the world

Close to God as I am to a perfect love and more
Love like that new love eternal

Brave and strong for myself and others
Free from guilt and shame

I am
One who has forgiven others

I am
One who has forgiven myself

Possessed of my own strong voice
I free my voice
I reclaim my voice
I am my voice and my voice is me and

I am
A song, A dance

I am art and artist deeply

I am life come more abundantly and
Blessed, blessed mother…
Inspired
Patient
Joyous
Teacher
Lover of knowledge, passing it on

Mother lover art woman wide open free

I am Divine

I am forgiven

I am here again forever

And this ring is a symbol of all that I am.

A FEW ADDITIONAL NOTES

"And we, having witnessed this commitment ceremony on this day, to this certificate set our hands."

If you are planning a ceremony with family and friends in attendance, there are a few additional (and fun) things to consider.

Will a spiritual counselor facilitate your ceremony? Will your friends be seated or will they stand with you to bear witness to your promises to self? Will you hire a photographer or will you ask friends to take pictures? Will you serve food? (There are additional pages in the appendix for those of you planning a more formal ceremony.)

The thought of serving food is almost enough to make me want to plan a recommitment ceremony with my friends and family in attendance. I envision an all night, pie-baking party – or a joyous potluck dinner. (Then again, I'm so private, and the experience was, for me, so personal, that when it was all said and done, I would probably choose to do it alone again!)

Whatever you do, be creative in involving your friends and soul mates in your day... or not. If you do involve them,

⋄ Have them bring bulbs, flowers, and plants for a garden that will symbolize the emergence and cultivation of your truest self. Dig up the earth beforehand and, as part of your ceremony, have everyone offer a word of love and support before putting their offering in the ground. After the ceremony add a stone or plaque commemorating the event, and watch your beautiful garden grow. (Nurturing your garden will be a good, tangible reminder that nurturing your commitment to self will take similar levels of care and concern.)

⋄ Have everyone write a wish for you on a piece of paper, tie it to a helium balloon and, after reading the wish out loud, release it.

⋄ Have a huge canvas and paints available, and encourage everyone to paint a picture or write a message, creating a huge collage on your behalf. Frame it and put it on your wall.

⋄ Have a calligrapher write out your promises on a big piece of fine paper. Have a floral, watercolor border added if you like. After your promises have been read aloud, sign your name to them as part of the ceremony. Once you have signed, have your guests sign as well.

If you like, the script – loosely based on the Quaker tradition – could read as follows:

PROMISES
"On this day, DATE, friends and family gathered in TOWN, STATE to witness NAME('s) commitment to him/her self.

In celebration and affirmation of my intent, I set my hand.

YOUR SIGNATURE

And we, having witnessed this commitment ceremony on this day, to this certificate set our hands.

GUEST SIGNATURES

Frame it and put it on your wall.

Finally, remember that you can perform a group ceremony with your best friends or with a women's group. Don't forget to write and share your experience, and send photos if you have them. I can't wait to hear all about it.

Wild hope,
Sara

Sara@dressringpromises.com
www.dressringpromises.com

Balsam Mountain Inn & Restaurant

68 Seven Springs Drive Balsam, North Carolina 28707
800.224.9498 – Email Us relax@balsaminn.com

NOTES

APPENDIX

For a more formal approach

All photos by Kate Crafton
Kate Crafton photography
http://katecrafton.blogspot.com/

THE COMMITMENT CEREMONY

Location/Site

Site Name _____ Contact _____

Address _____

Phone _____ Fax _____ Email _____

Reservation date and time _____ Capacity _____

Cost_____ Deposit _____ Balance _____

Officiant

Name _____

Address _____

Phone _____ Fax _____ Email _____

Order of Ceremony

_____

_____

_____

_____

_____

_____

_____

_____

Readings and Readers

_____

_____

_____

_____

_____

_____

_____

Music Selections

_____

_____

_____

_____

_____

_____

_____

_____

_____

Musicians

Name _____ Email _____

Address _____

Phone _____ Cost _____

Name _____ Email _____

Address _____

Phone _____ Cost _____

Name _____ Email _____

Address _____

Phone _____ Cost _____

Name _____ Email _____

Address _____

Phone _____ Cost _____

Name _____ Email _____

Address _____

Phone _____ Cost _____

PROGRAM

Program order and wording

_____

_____

_____

_____

_____

_____

_____

_____

_____

_____

_____

_____

_____

_____

_____

_____

_____

_____

DRESS

Purchased from _____

Phone _____ Fax _____ Email _____

Address _____

Manufacturer _____

Date ordered _____ Pickup _____

Deposit paid _____ Balance due _____ Total Cost _____

Fitting Schedule

Date_____ Time _____ Notes _____

Date_____ Time _____ Notes _____

Date_____ Time _____ Notes _____

Date_____ Time _____ Notes _____

ACCESSORIES

Accessory _____ Purchased from _____

Phone _____ Fax _____ Email _____

Address _____

Date ordered _____ Pickup _____

Deposit paid _____ Balance due _____ Total Cost_____

Accessory _____ Purchased from _____

Phone _____ Fax _____ Email _____

Address _____

Date ordered _____ Pickup _____

Deposit paid _____ Balance due _____ Total Cost_____

Accessory _____ Purchased from _____

Phone _____ Fax _____ Email _____

Address _____

Date ordered _____ Pickup _____

Deposit paid _____ Balance due _____ Total Cost_____

FLOWERS

Florist

Name _____ Contact _____

Address _____

Website _____

Phone _____ Fax _____ Email _____

Bouquet

Description _____

_____

_____

_____ Cost _____

Flowers for the Ceremony

Description _____

_____

_____

_____ Cost _____

RING

Purchased from _____

Phone _____ Fax _____ Email _____

Address _____

Manufacturer _____

Date ordered _____ Pickup _____

Deposit paid _____ Balance due _____ Total Cost_____

Notes

_____

_____

_____

_____

_____

_____

_____

_____

_____

_____

RENTAL ITEMS

Rental Company _____ Contact _____

Address _____

Phone _____ Fax _____ Email _____

Time and date of delivery _____

Items rented _____

_____

_____

_____

_____

_____

_____

_____

_____

_____

_____

_____

_____

Deposit paid _____ Balance due _____ Total Cost _____

THE RECEPTION

Location/Site

Site Name _____ Contact _____

Address _____

Phone _____ Fax _____ Email _____

Reservation date and time _____ Capacity _____

Cost _____ Deposit _____ Balance _____

Musicians

Name _____ Email _____

Address _____

Phone _____ Cost _____

Name _____ Email _____

Address _____

Phone _____ Cost _____

Name _____ Email _____

Address _____

Phone _____ Cost _____

RENTAL ITEMS

Rental Company _____ Contact _____

Address _____

Phone _____ Fax _____ Email _____

Time and date of delivery _____

Items rented _____

_____

_____

_____

_____

_____

_____

_____

_____

_____

_____

_____

_____

_____

Deposit paid _____ Balance due _____ Total Cost_____

FOOD

Catering Company

Name _____ Contact _____

Address/Website _____

Phone _____ Fax _____ Email _____

Final Guest count_____ Cost per person _____ Total cost _____

Number of servers _____ Cost per person _____ Total cost _____

Notes _____

Menu

Hors d'oeuvres _____

_____

_____

Accompaniments_____

_____

_____

Entrée _____

_____

_____

Desserts _____

_____

_____

Beverages

Name _____ Contact _____

Address/Website _____

Phone _____ Fax _____ Email _____

Beverages ordered_____

_____

Time and date of delivery _____Total Cost _____

Wedding Cake

Bakery _____ Contact _____

Address/Website _____

Phone _____ Fax _____ Email _____

Cake description_____

_____

Time and date of delivery _____Total Cost _____

(Or, have a potluck dinner. And don't forget the all-night, pie-baking party!)

RECEPTION FLOWERS

Head table arrangement _____

Cost _____

Table arrangement _____

_____

_____

Cost per table _____ Total Cost _____

Additional flowers for reception site _____

PHOTOGRAPHY

Name _____ Contact _____

Address/Website _____

Phone _____ Fax _____ Email _____

Cost _____ Booked from _____ to _____

INVITATIONS

Stationery

Name _____ Contact _____

Address/Website _____

Phone _____ Fax _____ Email _____

Description _____

Date ready _____ Picked up _____ Sent _____

Invitation Wording

_____

_____

_____

_____

_____

Response Card Wording

_____

_____

_____

_____

_____

GUEST LIST

Name _____ Invitation sent ☐

Address _____

City _____ State _____ Zip _____

Phone _____ Email _____

RSVP received ☐ Number attending _____ Gift _____ Thank you sent ☐

Name _____ Invitation sent ☐

Address _____

City _____ State _____ Zip _____

Phone _____ Email _____

RSVP received ☐ Number attending _____ Gift _____ Thank you sent ☐

Name _____ Invitation sent ☐

Address _____

City _____ State _____ Zip _____

Phone _____ Email _____

RSVP received ☐ Number attending _____ Gift _____ Thank you sent ☐

Name _____ Invitation sent ☐

Address _____

City _____ State _____ Zip _____

Phone _____ Email _____

RSVP received ☐ Number attending _____ Gift _____ Thank you sent ☐

Name _____ Invitation sent ☐

Address _____

City _____ State _____ Zip _____

Phone _____ Email _____

RSVP received ☐ Number attending _____ Gift _____ Thank you sent ☐

Name _____ Invitation sent ☐

Address _____

City _____ State _____ Zip _____

Phone _____ Email _____

RSVP received ☐ Number attending _____ Gift _____ Thank you sent ☐

Name _____ Invitation sent ☐

Address _____

City _____ State _____ Zip _____

Phone _____ Email _____

RSVP received ☐ Number attending _____ Gift _____ Thank you sent ☐

Name _____ Invitation sent □

Address _____

City _____ State _____ Zip _____

Phone _____ Email _____

RSVP received □ Number attending _____ Gift _____ Thank you sent □

Name _____ Invitation sent □

Address _____

City _____ State _____ Zip _____

Phone _____ Email _____

RSVP received □ Number attending _____ Gift _____ Thank you sent □

Name _____ Invitation sent □

Address _____

City _____ State _____ Zip _____

Phone _____ Email _____

RSVP received □ Number attending _____ Gift _____ Thank you sent □

Name _____ Invitation sent □

Address _____

City _____ State _____ Zip _____

Phone _____ Email _____

RSVP received □ Number attending _____ Gift _____ Thank you sent □

Name _____ Invitation sent ☐

Address _____

City _____ State _____ Zip _____

Phone _____ Email _____

RSVP received ☐ Number attending _____ Gift _____ Thank you sent ☐

Name _____ Invitation sent ☐

Address _____

City _____ State _____ Zip _____

Phone _____ Email _____

RSVP received ☐ Number attending _____ Gift _____ Thank you sent ☐

Name _____ Invitation sent ☐

Address _____

City _____ State _____ Zip _____

Phone _____ Email _____

RSVP received ☐ Number attending _____ Gift _____ Thank you sent ☐

Name _____ Invitation sent ☐

Address _____

City _____ State _____ Zip _____

Phone _____ Email _____

RSVP received ☐ Number attending _____ Gift _____ Thank you sent ☐

Name _____ Invitation sent ☐

Address _____

City _____ State _____ Zip _____

Phone _____ Email _____

RSVP received ☐ Number attending _____ Gift _____ Thank you sent ☐

Name _____ Invitation sent ☐

Address _____

City _____ State _____ Zip _____

Phone _____ Email _____

RSVP received ☐ Number attending _____ Gift _____ Thank you sent ☐

Name _____ Invitation sent ☐

Address _____

City _____ State _____ Zip _____

Phone _____ Email _____

RSVP received ☐ Number attending _____ Gift _____ Thank you sent ☐

Name _____ Invitation sent ☐

Address _____

City _____ State _____ Zip _____

Phone _____ Email _____

RSVP received ☐ Number attending _____ Gift _____ Thank you sent ☐

Name _____ Invitation sent ☐

Address _____

City _____ State _____ Zip _____

Phone _____ Email _____

RSVP received ☐ Number attending _____ Gift _____ Thank you sent ☐

Name _____ Invitation sent ☐

Address _____

City _____ State _____ Zip _____

Phone _____ Email _____

RSVP received ☐ Number attending _____ Gift _____ Thank you sent ☐

Name _____ Invitation sent ☐

Address _____

City _____ State _____ Zip _____

Phone _____ Email _____

RSVP received ☐ Number attending _____ Gift _____ Thank you sent ☐

Name _____ Invitation sent ☐

Address _____

City _____ State _____ Zip _____

Phone _____ Email _____

RSVP received ☐ Number attending _____ Gift _____ Thank you sent ☐

Name _____ Invitation sent ☐

Address _____

City _____ State _____ Zip _____

Phone _____ Email _____

RSVP received ☐ Number attending _____ Gift _____ Thank you sent ☐

Name _____ Invitation sent ☐

Address _____

City _____ State _____ Zip _____

Phone _____ Email _____

RSVP received ☐ Number attending _____ Gift _____ Thank you sent ☐

Name _____ Invitation sent ☐

Address _____

City _____ State _____ Zip _____

Phone _____ Email _____

RSVP received ☐ Number attending _____ Gift _____ Thank you sent ☐

Name _____ Invitation sent ☐

Address _____

City _____ State _____ Zip _____

Phone _____ Email _____

RSVP received ☐ Number attending _____ Gift _____ Thank you sent ☐

COLLAGE

On this and the following pages, cut and paste pictures
that capture the image you have of your special day.

ABOUT THE AUTHOR

photo by Elizabeth Jackson

Sara Sharpe is an award-winning actress, writer and social entrepreneur from Nashville, Tennessee. She is the sole proprietor of SHARPE Communication, offering communication and presentation skills for women in a safe and nurturing environment, with the express purpose of encouraging women to strengthen their voices, speak truth to power, and tell the stories that inspire them to take action on behalf of their own lives or someone else's. (www.sharpecommunication.com). She is also the co-founder and former Artistic Director of the BroadAxe Theatre (Best New Theatre Company, 2001 Nashville Scene), Nashville's most political theatre, and one which joins the long tradition of popular theatres working to unravel and express the root causes of social and political ills.

Sara is the creator of FESTIVE EVOLUTION: Art and Activism in the Twenty-first Century, an organization dedicated to helping artists mobilize their art and fan base for social and political change through ongoing educational programs and activities. Festive Evolution proudly presents Sara's documentary/docudrama FAIRVIEW: An American Conversation. www.thefairviewproject.com. Currently, Sara and

Fest Ev host monthly ARTemis meetings for female artists, in and around the Nashville area, involved in social change. See www.festiveevolution.com for more information. Sara is the recipient of the NCADP Community Service Award. She can be reached at Sara@dressringpromises.com.

ACKNOWLEDGEMENTS

I find I've an inordinate number of people to thank for so small a book. This makes sense, I suppose, in that this book represents years of painstaking growth and discovery – the kind that requires the love and support of a great many friends and loved ones.

In terms of the book itself, there are two women whom I wish to thank especially; women without whom this beloved little book would never have had a life beyond my personal book shelf; Elizabeth Jackson, who fell in love with the book and who encouraged me to make it available to others, and author DJ Anderson, who convinced me that I could turn the handmade version into a "real" book. DJ took it upon herself to design the book you're holding, and to make it available on Amazon. Thanks also to DJ's daughter, Ariel, who built the lovely website: www.dresssringpromises.com.

Thanks to photographer Kate Crafton, who opened her catalog and allowed me to choose whatever photos I wanted for this project.

In terms of the journey itself, thanks to thoroughly adored friends both old and new: Carolyn, Chris, Holly A., Holly B., Jane, Joanne, Kim, Maryanna, Pru, Sharon S. and my girls at the DAC, as well as the "chicks for peace" and the inestimable ARTemis group. Special thanks to Carlene and Jolie for quarterly, 48-hour eat/talk/dream fests that keep me both sane and inspired, and to Laura and Lori (aka "the mean girls") for years of lunches, laughter and tears. Thanks to Amy for being Amy, and for knowing my story and calling me "the most freakishly sane person" she's ever met. (I've not been accused of that before or since.) Thanks to Ms. Sunnye, for insisting that I tell the story (I've started, see?!) and special thanks to Paige for the beautiful poem.

Thanks to Lynne Forest for lighting our path on a regular basis, and to Liz and Don Klinefelter, as well as Anna, Tommy and Jade Chastain for help and encouragement. I am thoroughly convinced that I have the best family in the world and I love you all beyond measure.

Thanks to Jamie for … everything. Words fail me. Sometimes words are not enough.

Most of all, thanks to Trenna and Jacob for bearing with me while I learned (the hard way) to love, honor and care for myself, so that I might better love, honor and care for them.

Finally.

"Let me teach your heart to love, as I will teach my own…" Dar Williams.

Made in the USA
San Bernardino, CA
22 December 2014